Easy-Step

Wallpapering

Contents

Introduction 4

Planning and Choosing Materials 7
  1 Select materials
  2 Choose a pattern
  3 Gather tools
  4 Estimate materials

Preparing Walls 15
  1 Remove fixtures
  2 Strip off old wallcovering
  3 Patch and smooth walls
  4 Prime or clean walls
  5 Set up the work site
  6 Center on a focal point . . .
     . . . or choose a mismatch spot
  7 Plan for each sheet

Hanging the First Sheets 27
  1 Apply primer/sealer
  2 Draw a plumb line
  3 Cut the first sheet
  4 Cut the next sheets
  5 Plan for large patterns
  6 Paste and book
  7 Hang and smooth
  8 Choose a seam technique

Corners and Obstacles 39
1 Trim the sheets
2 Doors and windows
3 Inside corners
4 Outside corners
5 Outlets and pipes
6 Recessed windows

Special Applications 49
1 Cover an electrical plate
2 Archway
3 Stairway
4 Dormer
5 Ceiling
6 Borders

Repairs 61
1 Fix a seam
2 Flatten a bubble
3 Patch a damaged area

U.S./Metric Measure Conversions 64

Introduction

Wallpapering is one of the quickest ways
to revamp a room. A vast range of colors,
patterns, and textures is available to establish
the style and mood you desire. Hundreds of
new patterns hit the market each year, from
vintage designs that evoke a style from the past, to
up-to-the-minute patterns as contemporary
as a magazine ad. Because many wallcoverings are
made with materials that are easy to maintain—even
in bathrooms and children's rooms—wallcoverings
can be as utilitarian as they are stylish.

Just about anyone with patience, basic how-to skills,
and a few essential tools can learn to wallpaper.
The key to successful wallpapering is a methodical
approach. That means planning ahead and taking
the time to work step-by-step. Whether you are
covering a plain wall or have a more complex project
involving corners and obstacles, *Wallpapering* gives
you easy-to-understand guidance for doing the job
yourself. To get an overview that will help you
avoid missteps and false starts, read the entire book
before beginning the project. Once you start, keep
Wallpapering close at hand—it's designed to be
a quick reference while the work is under way.

Before you begin, try to develop a master decorating plan that includes not only the room you plan to wallpaper, but also the adjoining rooms. Choose wallcovering and fabrics first—paint for the walls, ceiling, and trim can be mixed to complement them. Expect to take a good deal of time choosing the wallcovering. Keep in mind that most wallcoverings will not be in stock and will have to be ordered. Allow at least a week for delivery. Then set aside a weekend and look forward to transforming the room!

Planning and Choosing Materials

Select materials

Wallcoverings are made from a variety of materials. In making a selection, consider not only looks, but also washability and ease of installation. Avoid wallcoverings that wrinkle easily. Do not count on wallcovering to hide serious flaws in the walls. The thinner and shinier the material, the more it will show imperfections. Avoid wallpaper with selvage edges that must be trimmed before installing.

Wallcovering Materials

Type	Advantage	Disadvantage
Printed paper	Most common type, available in a wide variety of patterns and prices.	Only light soil can be washed off—not scrubbable.
Vinyl-coated paper or cloth	Easy to apply. Scrubbable, stain-resistant, and difficult to tear. Thick and textured vinyl can cover wall flaws well.	Vinyl look can seem "cold" for some living areas.
Foil	Often made with polyester film rather than true foil. Brightens a room by reflecting light.	Very difficult to apply. Will magnify even the smallest flaws in the surface. Tears are difficult to mend.
Grass cloth	Made with attractive natural plant fibers. Covers wall flaws well. Easy to apply.	Difficult to clean—soaking with water can damage the fibers.
Flocked	These use nylon or rayon for a velvet effect. Available on paper, vinyl, or foil.	Requires extra care in installation. Not durable or washable—flocking is easily damaged.
Fabrics	A versatile option, often very inexpensive. Easy to apply if there is no pattern to match.	Difficult to wash. Spraying with a protective coating changes its color. Stretches during application.

Choose a pattern

Patterned or textured wallcoverings must be hung so that their edges match. Some patterns are easier to match than others. *Random texture* wallcoverings can be joined at any point, because there is no pattern to be carried through. *Small-pattern* coverings are more demanding. They need to be aligned exactly, which means sliding the material up or down a few inches until the pattern matches. As a result, some of the wallcovering is trimmed off and discarded.

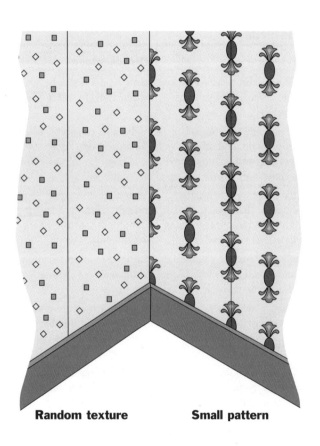

Random texture   **Small pattern**

Random match patterns are vertical. The pattern does not have to be aligned horizontally, so two sheets can be joined together at any point. On the other hand, matching a *large pattern* results in as much as 15-percent waste, because a sheet may have to be moved a foot or so up or down to make a match. Some large patterns cause more waste than others. To save yourself extra work and material, select a pattern that requires the least amount of shifting.

Random match   **Large pattern**

3 Gather tools

Although wallpapering can be done with common tools that you may already have—level, yardstick, scissors, and sponge, for instance—some specialized tools will make the work go easier and produce a better-looking job. These include a *bubble stick*, which is marked like a yardstick and is easier to handle than a carpenter's level, and wallpaper scissors, which are longer and sharper than regular scissors.

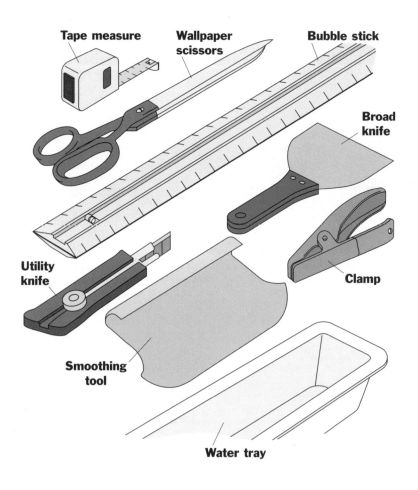

Tape measure **Wallpaper scissors** **Bubble stick**

Broad knife

Utility knife **Clamp**

Smoothing tool

Water tray

Knife blades must be razor sharp to avoid tearing the material, so have lots of extra blades on hand. Smoothing tools eliminate air trapped under the wallcovering that will lead to unsightly bubbles (sometimes called blisters). Keep all tools clean. Choose adhesive and primer/sealer that is made for the job at hand. For instance, grass cloth and fabric require a clear adhesive. Other adhesives are sold specifically for applying vinyl over vinyl.

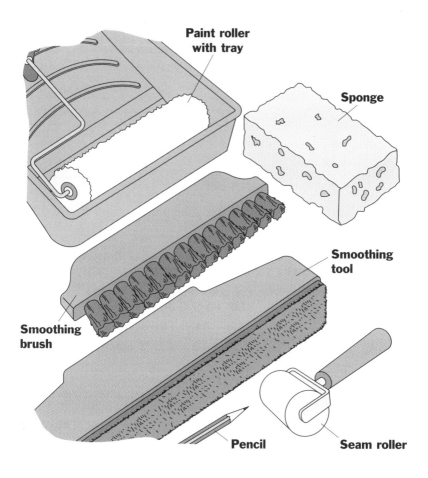

Paint roller with tray

Sponge

Smoothing tool

Smoothing brush

Pencil

Seam roller

4

Estimate materials

To estimate materials, determine the square footage of each wall by multiplying the height by the width. (For the height, measure from baseboard to ceiling. If using a large pattern, add at least 6 inches as additional waste allowance.) Total the square footage of the walls. If using *American* rolls, divide by 30 to get the number of single rolls you will need (a standard single roll contains 36 square feet; dividing by 30 allows for normal waste). Subtract the total area of doors and windows.

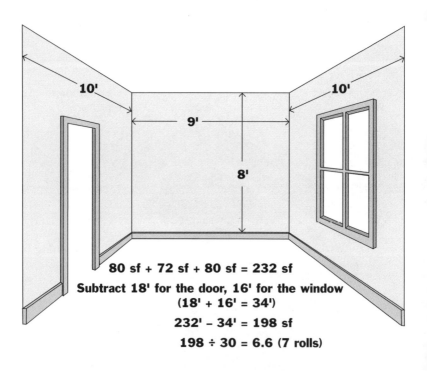

80 sf + 72 sf + 80 sf = 232 sf
Subtract 18' for the door, 16' for the window
(18' + 16' = 34')
232' − 34' = 198 sf
198 ÷ 30 = 6.6 (7 rolls)

TIP: If using *European* rolls (28 square feet per roll), divide the total square footage by 22 to allow for waste.

For a more accurate estimate, count the sheets. To do so, find out how wide and how long the roll will be (you will probably buy double rolls, which offer twice the coverage of single rolls). Mark the location of each sheet on the wall (see page 24), and calculate the length of material needed. With a large pattern, add to the height of the wall the distance between the repeats. (If the pattern repeats every 20 inches and the wall is 96 inches high, plan for sheets 116 inches long).

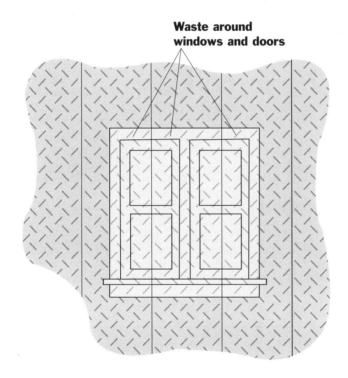

**Waste around
windows and doors**

TIP: Allow for mistakes by ordering
10–20 percent extra wallcovering.
Whole rolls can usually be returned
if the wrapping is unopened.

1 Remove fixtures

Work your way around the room, removing electrical outlet and switch covers, light fixtures, nails, brackets—anything that will get in the way of wallpapering. Be systematic so that nothing is left that protrudes from the wall—it's no fun discovering an obstruction *after* wallcovering has been applied.

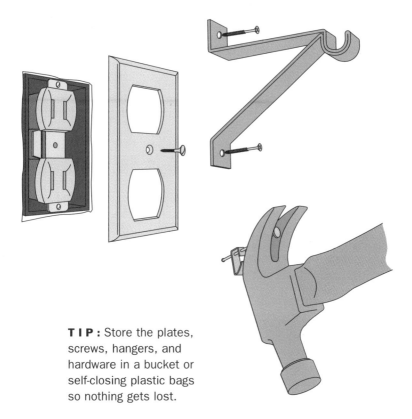

TIP: Store the plates, screws, hangers, and hardware in a bucket or self-closing plastic bags so nothing gets lost.

2 Strip off old wallcovering

If the existing wallcovering is well adhered and very smooth, it can be primed and papered over, but usually it's best to remove old material. Some types come off simply by slipping a broad knife underneath and pulling the wallcovering off. With a porous material (paper, cloth, or fiber), use removal solution or rent a wallpaper steamer. As the paste softens, the covering comes off more or less easily with a broad knife.

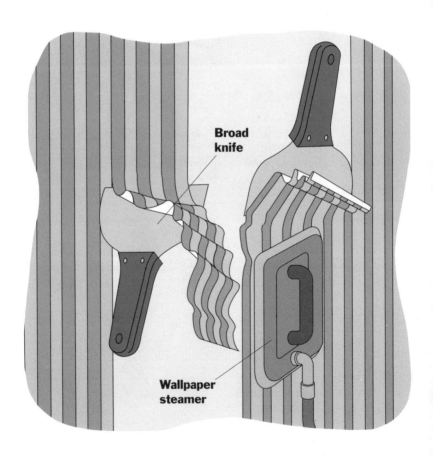

Broad knife

Wallpaper steamer

If the wallcovering is tightly adhered and nonporous (vinyl, foil, painted-over material), the surface must be perforated to allow the remover to penetrate. Use a perforation tool to break the surface of the wallcovering without harming the underlying plaster or wallboard. Roll it back and forth on a section of wall, then apply the removal solution with a sponge or sprayer, according to manufacturer's directions. Scrape off the covering with a broad knife.

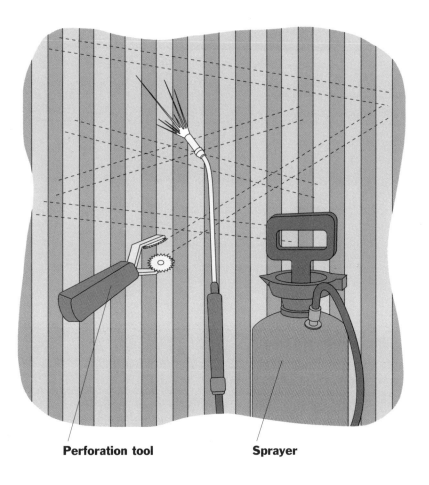

Perforation tool   **Sprayer**

3 Patch and smooth walls

Scrape or pry off any loose material from the wall. Fill small holes with joint compound or vinyl spackling compound, repeating applications until smooth. For large cracks in wallboard or plaster, scrape and apply mesh tape before spackling. Allow the area to dry, scrape off ridges and bumps, and apply more coats if necessary.

Joint compound or
vinyl spackling compound

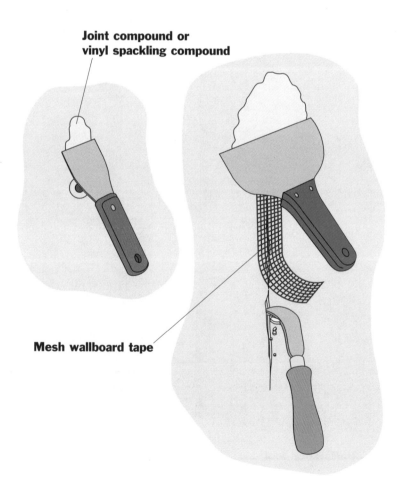

Mesh wallboard tape

After the patching compound is completely dry, sand it smooth, using a large sanding block or pole sander. Don't just eyeball the wall to see if it's smooth. Run your hand over the whole surface to feel for bumps and valleys. Unless you will be using a coarse wallcovering, imperfections may become more apparent after you cover them.

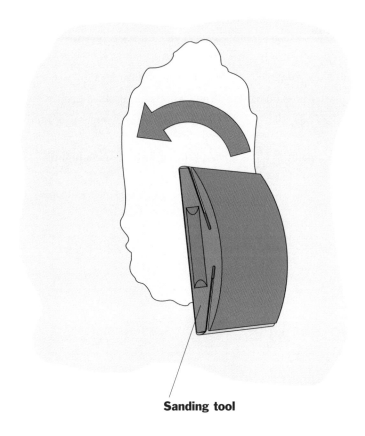

Sanding tool

Prime or clean walls

Once the walls are smooth and dry, prepare them for wallpapering. Porous walls must be primed so they won't absorb too much paste. If the walls have a shiny surface, degloss them so the glue will adhere. Specific conditions and remedies include the following:

Sealing Walls

Condition	Procedure
Flat or shiny latex paint	Lightly sand the surface
Unpainted plaster or wallboard	Prime with latex or alkyd primer
Flat oil-based paint	Clean with a mild detergent solution and rinse
Glossy oil-based paint	Sand the surface, or use a liquid deglosser
Stained areas	Apply alcohol-based primer formulated for hiding stains

Set up the work site

Clear the area of all furniture and obstacles—
wallpapering requires plenty of elbow room.
Spread out a drop cloth to protect the floor. Set
up a large table, or lay a sheet of plywood on
two sawhorses. Have a large garbage can handy and at least
one sturdy ladder tall enough to enable you to work com-
fortably at ceiling height.

Plenty of light   **Drop cloth**

Large work   **Clean**   **Garbage can**
surface   **water**

21

6 Center on a focal point . . .

To avoid awkward or unsightly seams, anticipate the location of every sheet of wallcovering. Begin with the wall area most likely to attract attention. This may be above a mantle, the center of the wall that people see when first entering the room, or a center point between two windows. Center the seam, or center the sheet. You may have to experiment with several plans before you figure out where to begin. Avoid sheets less than 6 inches wide at corners.

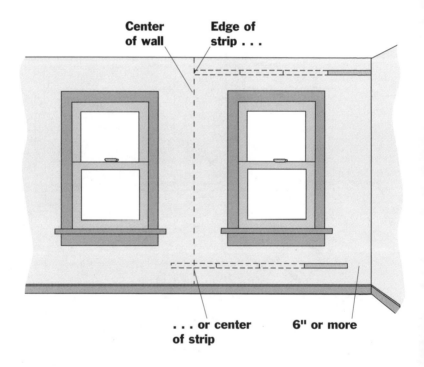

Center of wall

Edge of strip . . .

. . . or center of strip

6" or more

. . . or choose a mismatch spot

If you will be wallpapering all the walls in a room, there will likely be a mismatch spot—a place where one sheet will be narrower and the patterns will not match at the seam. Place the mismatch where it will be least noticeable—above the entry door or at an inside corner.

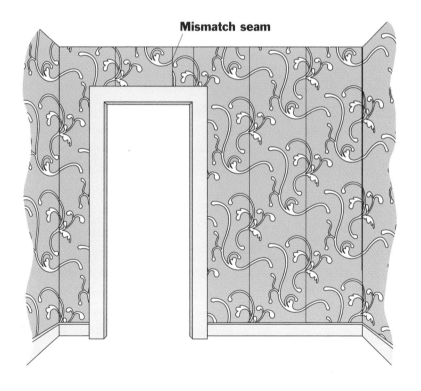

Mismatch seam

Plan for each sheet

Marking the walls lightly with a pencil, lay out the entire job. This takes time, but it will help you avoid missteps that will slow you down and make the job look unprofessional. If you find that you will need sheets less than 6 inches wide along the sides of windows or doors, rework the plan.

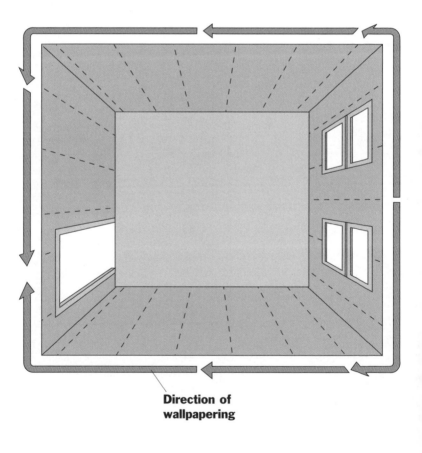

Direction of wallpapering

If you discover that a seam will fall almost exactly on a corner, rework the layout. Wallcovering must wrap around corners. Allow at least a 1½-inch overlap for outside corners and ¼ inch for inside corners (measure at the ceiling line, midpoint, and baseboard and add ¼ inch to the largest measurement). The overlap helps ensure that the glue will adhere and compensates for slightly out-of-plumb corners.

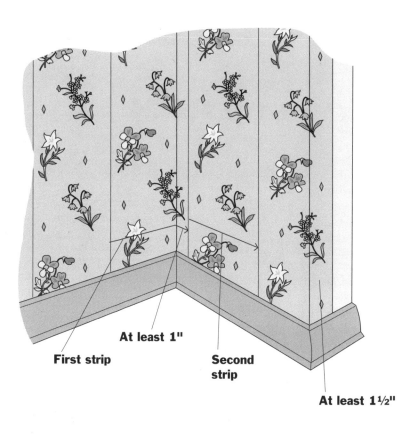

At least 1"

First strip

Second strip

At least 1½"

Hanging the First Sheets

1 Apply primer/sealer

Coat the wall with premixed primer/sealer
(available in oil- and acrylic-based formulas)
made specifically for use under wallcoverings.
This coating creates a surface film that improves
adhesion. Apply it to the entire wall surface with a roller
or broad brush and allow the wall to dry completely. A pig-
mented oil-based primer/sealer prevents paint colors from
showing through lightweight coverings.

Broad brush

2 Draw a plumb line

To ensure that the first sheet is plumb, make a mark ¼ inch past the layout mark so you will be able to see it when the sheet is put up. (This also ensures that the mark will not show if the seam is not tight.) Hold a bubble stick or level firmly to the mark. Center the bubble and carefully draw a faint plumb line from the ceiling to the baseboard.

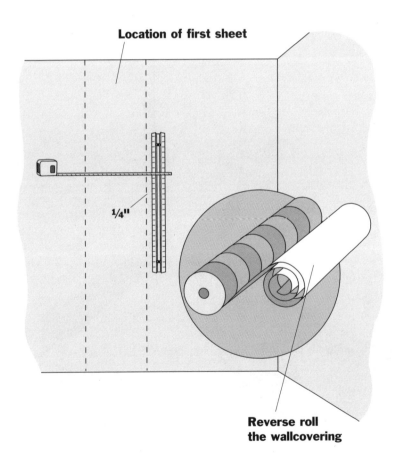

Location of first sheet

¼"

Reverse roll
the wallcovering

Cut the first sheet

Before cutting, unroll each wallcovering roll and reroll it backward so the unpatterned side is facing out. Inspect the surface for flaws as you do this. Return any unsatisfactory sheets to the store. Unroll the first roll of material again and stack it accordion-style on the floor at the foot of the work table. Pull the end of the roll onto the table and cut the first sheet. It should be at least 4 inches longer than the measured distance between ceiling and baseboard.

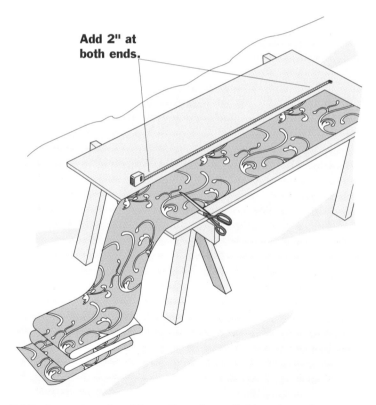

Add 2" at both ends.

T I P : Inspect each roll for pattern flaws, flaking pigment, and inconsistently textured vinyl coating. Check that the dye lot number is the same on all rolls—otherwise, there could be slight color variations.

Cut the next sheets

Align the next sheet so the pattern matches that of the first sheet. Cut it, leaving approximately 2 inches at the top and bottom for waste. If the wallcovering has a pattern that must be matched, stay one sheet ahead of the pasting process (see page 32), so you always have a dry sheet with which to align the next.

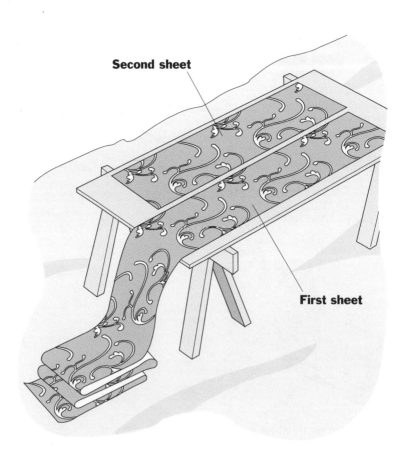

Second sheet

First sheet

5 Plan for large patterns

If using a large pattern, cut the first sheet a foot longer than needed. Hold it in place and adjust up or down according to what looks best. Mark the sheet lightly at the ceiling and baseboard and then trim it about 2 inches too long on both ends. On the table, align the next sheet against it, and cut it to the same length. Cut a third sheet aligned to the second, and roll and store the sheets carefully, keeping them in order.

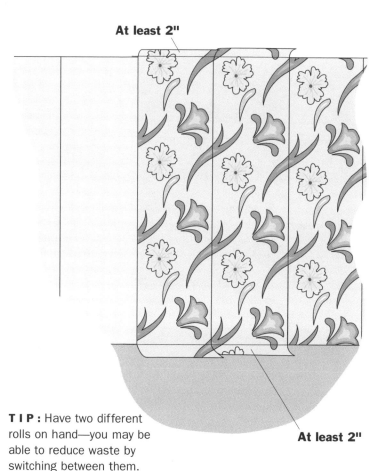

At least 2"

At least 2"

T I P : Have two different rolls on hand—you may be able to reduce waste by switching between them.

6 Paste and book

If you are using prepasted material, half-fill the water tray with lukewarm water and place it on the floor near where the sheet will be hung. Roll the sheet, pattern side in, and place it in the tray. Time the soaking according to manufacturer's instructions. If you are using paste, place the sheet upside-down on the table and apply the paste evenly with a paint roller. (Keep the table clean by covering it with plastic and wiping off excess paste after each sheet.)

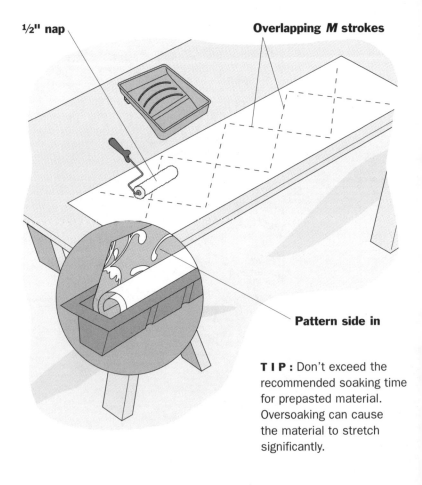

½" nap

Overlapping *M* strokes

Pattern side in

TIP : Don't exceed the recommended soaking time for prepasted material. Oversoaking can cause the material to stretch significantly.

After pasting, *book* the sheet by folding both ends inward so they nearly meet. Let the booked sheet sit for about 10 minutes. Booking helps spread the paste evenly and keeps the material wet so that it can soften and expand to its fullest dimensions. For easier handling, roll booked material as shown.

7

Hang and smooth

Pick up the booked material and climb the ladder. Unfold the top section and, taking care to avoid wrinkles, place it against the wall. Smooth the sheet gently in place. Check the plumb line—the material should be uniformly ¼ inch away. If not lined up, lift the material and shift it. When the upper part of the sheet is in position, flatten it on the wall with the smoothing brush, lightly stroking from the center outward.

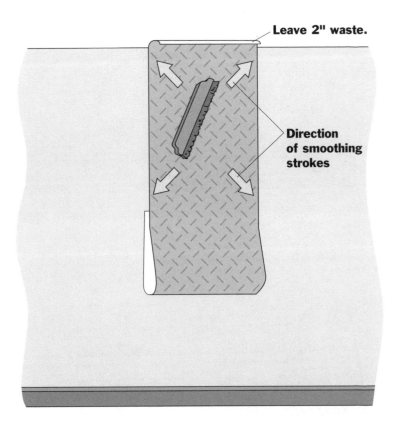

Leave 2" waste.

Direction of smoothing strokes

Pull out the bottom fold and slide the material into position. Check for plumb and adjust as necessary. Continue smoothing with the brush, working outward from the middle. Next smooth the sheet with a damp sponge, starting in the center and working outward. Wipe off excess paste, rinsing the sponge regularly. Do not trim the top and bottom until after you have hung the next sheet.

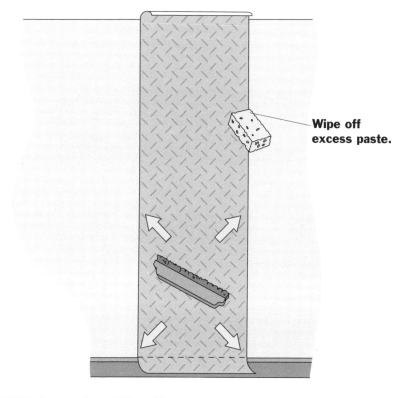

Wipe off excess paste.

T I P : Inspect for bubbles with a strong, glancing light, held at several different angles. Smooth out bubbles with the sponge.

Choose a seam technique

The most common of the four basic seam techniques is the *butt seam*—one sheet pushed against another and the seam rolled. A *spring-loaded seam* is a variation of the butt seam, used to ensure that the sheets are tightly joined. Lap one sheet over the other by about 1/64 inch and let it set for a few minutes. Then gently work the overlapping sheet with the palms of your hands and let it spring back into place.

Butt seam

Spring-loaded seam

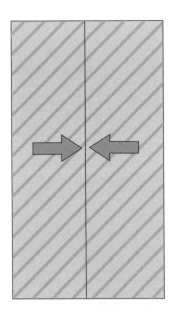

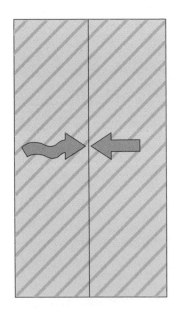

The *lap seam* is used at corners or at the mismatch spot. If you have random match or random texture wallcovering, use the lap seam to realign out-of-plumb sheets. Allow one sheet to overlap the other by about ¼ inch. To make a *double-cut seam*, first overlap the sheets, then make a single straight cut that goes through both sheets. Remove the scraps and push the sheets together.

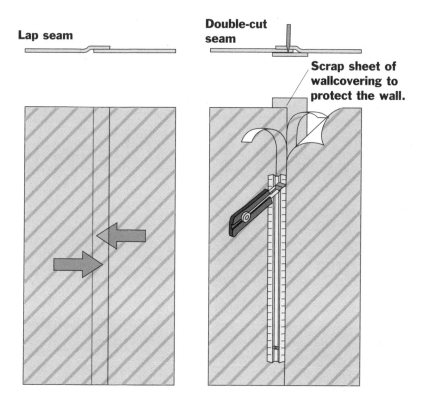

Lap seam

Double-cut seam

Scrap sheet of wallcovering to protect the wall.

Trim the sheets

To trim wallcovering in place, press the edge of a broad knife into the corner. This makes a crease and holds the material firmly. Take care not to tear the material. Hold the broad knife in place as a guide for the utility knife. To avoid ragged cuts, leave the utility knife in place as you move the broad knife. Or use the broad knife to make a crease, pull the material away, and cut it with scissors.

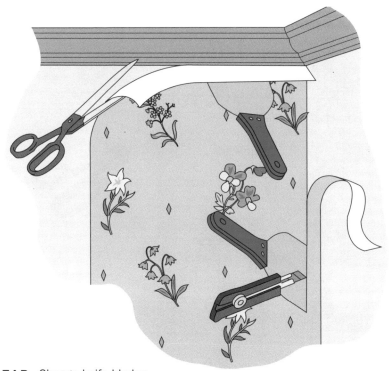

TIP: Change knife blades often—don't wait until a dull blade tears the material.

Doers and windows

2

To wallpaper around doors and windows that
have molding, first press the wallcovering in
place. Make a tight seam with the adjacent sheet.
Smooth the material as close to the molding as
possible without tearing the sheet. Then, with a utility knife
or scissors, make a 45-degree cut at each corner, ending
at the outermost corner of the molding. Smooth the material
closer to the molding. Finally, use the broad knife and utility
knife or scissors to trim the wallcovering along the edge of
the molding.

**Angle cut ends at outside
corner of molding**

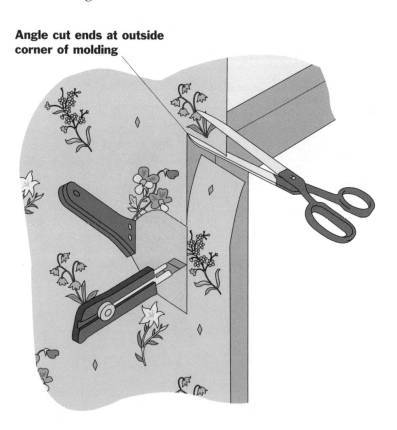

Windowsills (also called window stools) are often difficult to trim. Because sills stick out so far, it's easy to tear the material while trying to smooth and trim it. Cut the initial slit for the sill in two or three gradual steps to avoid over-cutting. Don't press the material against the wall too close to the sill. Make a series of small slits around a round-edged sill. Then press the material against the molding and do the final trimming.

Multiple slits for round edge

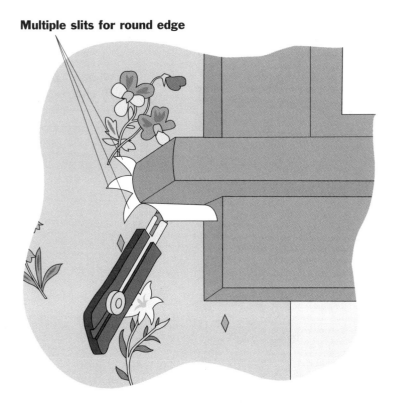

Inside corners

Corners are rarely plumb and perfectly straight. To avoid wrinkling, cover corners with over-lapping sheets and seam them to one side of the corner. Begin by cutting a sheet to the height of the wall plus 2 inches at the top and bottom. Measure the distance to the corner at several places, and cut the sheet so that it extends beyond the corner at least ¼ inch. Hang this sheet (sheet A). It will turn the corner and overlap onto the next wall.

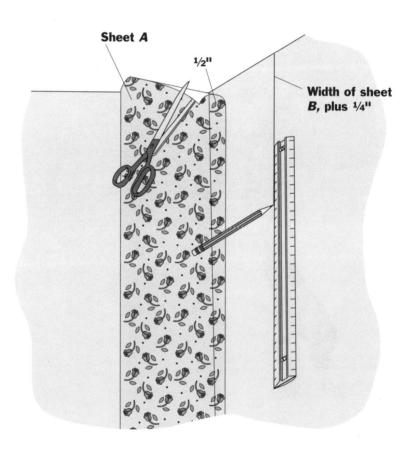

Sheet **A**

½"

Width of sheet B, plus ¼"

Measure the width of the sheet left over from the lengthwise cut (sheet *B*) and add ¼ inch. Measure this distance from the corner onto the uncovered wall, and draw a plumb line from ceiling to floor (see page 28). Install sheet *B*, overlapping it onto sheet *A* and keeping it evenly aligned along the plumb line. Leave the overlap, or use the double-cut seam technique (see page 37).

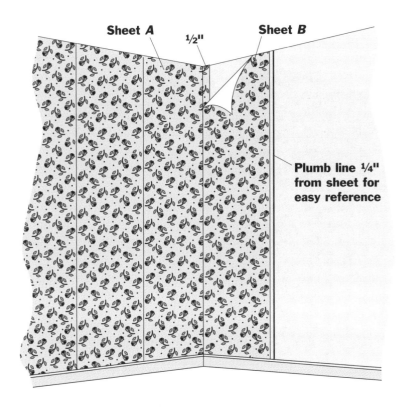

Sheet *A*   ½"   **Sheet *B***

**Plumb line ¼"
from sheet for
easy reference**

Outside corners

Outside corners are often less of a problem than inside corners—you may be able to simply wrap a full sheet without going out of plumb. If the corner is not plumb, use the same technique as for an inside corner, but cut sheet *A* to overlap the corner anywhere from 1½ to 6 inches. For either technique, cut slits at the top and bottom of the sheet, at the corner, to keep the material from tearing.

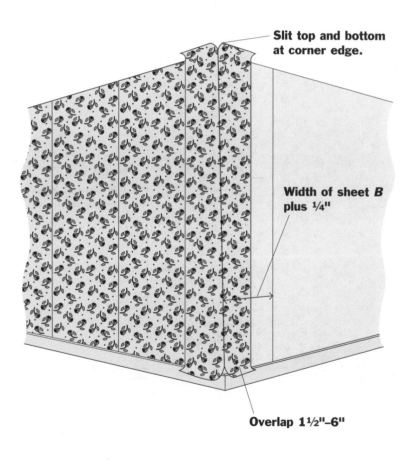

Slit top and bottom at corner edge.

Width of sheet *B* plus ¼"

Overlap 1½"–6"

Outlets and pipes

For electrical outlets, cover the prong slots with strips of electrical tape. Wallpaper over a receptacle (outlet, switch, or light fixture) loosely, then cut four angled slits from the center, each ending at the outside corner of the electrical box. Smooth the material down, then cut out the opening. For pipes, measure from the seam edge and make a slit so that you can slide the sheet into place. Trim around the pipe, and brush smooth.

**Slide escutcheon
away from wall.**

Recessed windows

To cover a recessed window, hang a full sheet
of wallcovering in place, allowing it to overhang
the recess. Cut the overhanging section as shown,
leaving a ½-inch flap along the vertical edge and
a full flap to cover the sill of the recess.

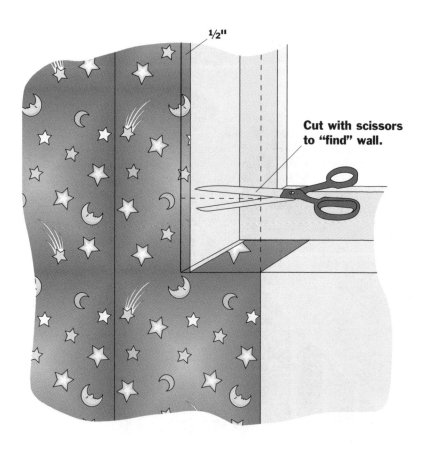

½"

Cut with scissors
to "find" wall.

Cut a strip to cover the inside face of the recessed area so
it will overlap 1 inch at the top and bottom. Trim it ¼ inch
narrower than the recess. If using patterned material, align
the sheet before trimming to make sure the pattern matches.
Hang the sheet so that both the bottom and top overlap ½
inch. Paste it and smooth it into place. (If the wallcovering
is vinyl, use vinyl-on-vinyl adhesive where it laps over the
first sheet.)

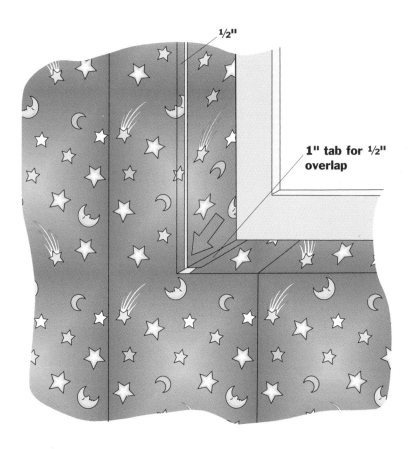

½"

1" tab for ½"
overlap

Special Applications

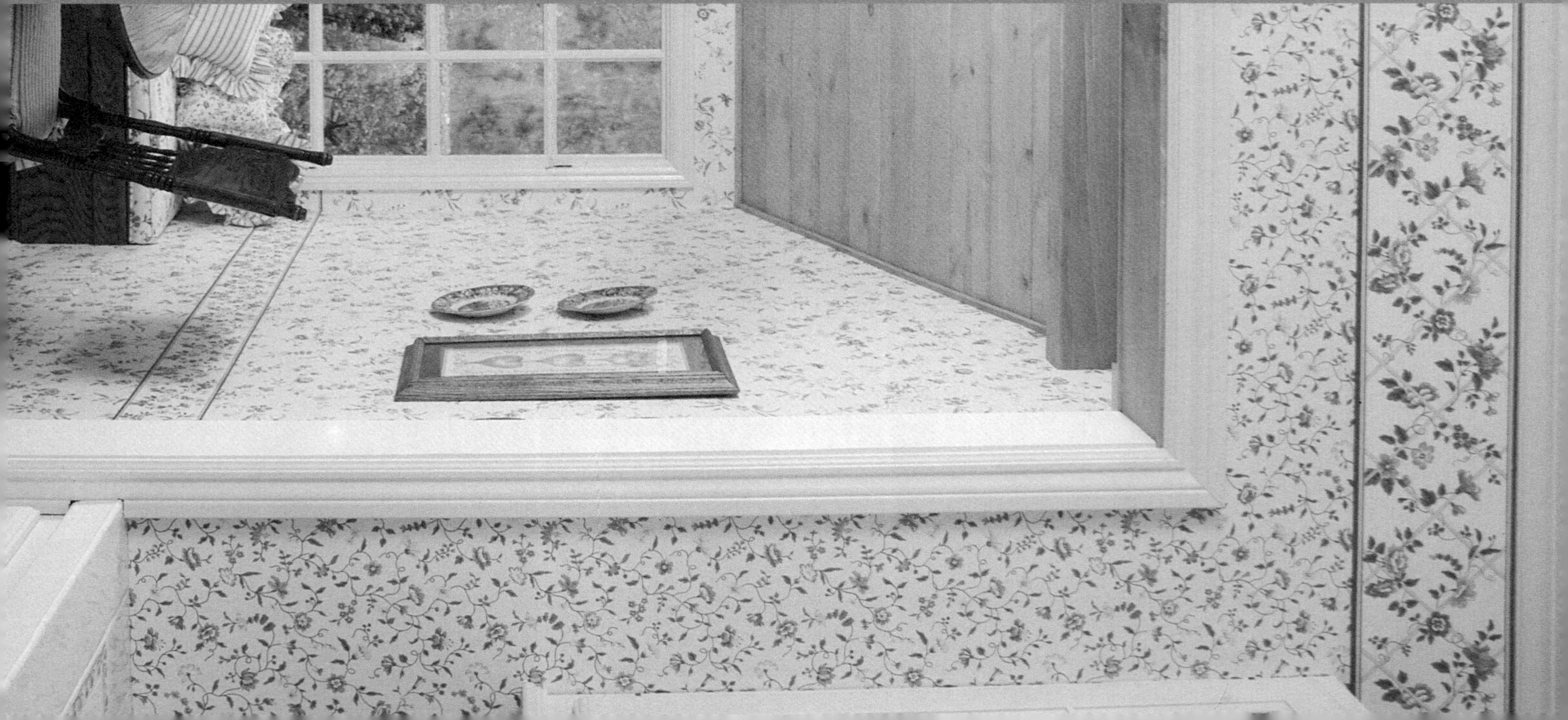

Cover an electrical plate

To cover an electrical plate so it blends in with the wall, put the plate in place, and position a scrap of wallcovering against it so the pattern matches. Crease the material against the plate to mark its position, then trim the corners as shown. Sand the plate with 120-grit sandpaper and paste the wallcovering on the plate.

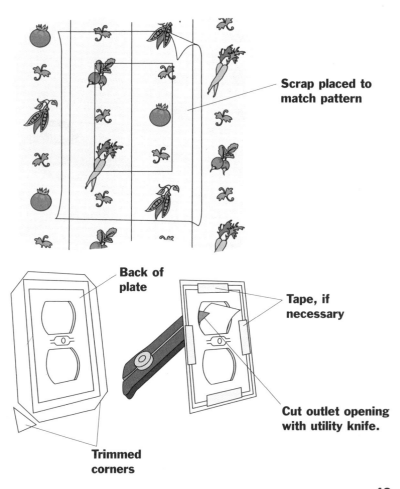

Scrap placed to match pattern

Back of plate

Tape, if necessary

Cut outlet opening with utility knife.

Trimmed corners

Archway

To cover a curved archway, first install sheets of wallcovering, allowing them to overhang the arch. Let the paste set but not completely dry, and trim the excess material so it overlaps the edge of the archway by 2 inches.

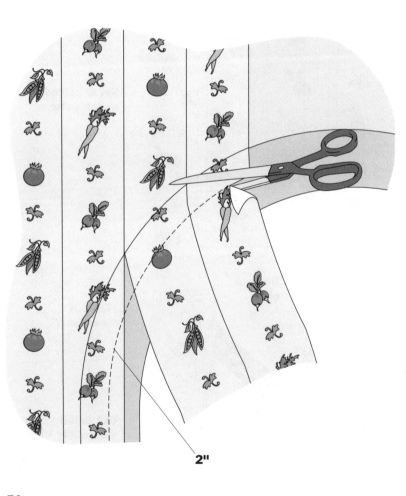

2"

Make a series of triangular cuts into the overlap. The tip of each triangle should come to within ⅛ inch of the edge of the arch. Paste the "teeth" onto the archway and allow them to set. Trim the teeth with a utility knife, so they overlap by about ½ inch. Cut a strip of wallcovering ¼ inch narrower than the archway (to avoid peeling) and paste it onto the underside of the archway.

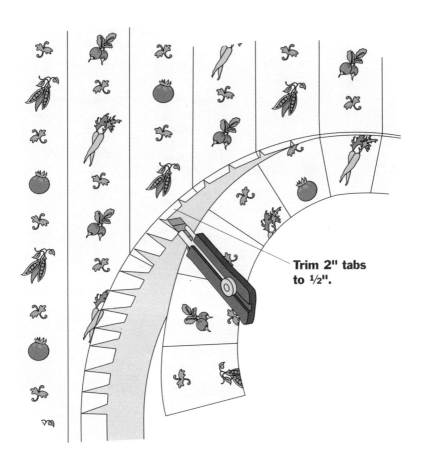

Trim 2" tabs to ½".

Stairway

Set up sturdy scaffolding and have a helper on hand. Plan for each sheet, laying out the job in advance. As you work down the stairway, measure the length of each sheet, taking care to measure the *longest* side and add 2 inches to each end. Draw plumb lines for the well wall and the head wall, as shown. Hang the longer sheets with one person working on top and one on the bottom.

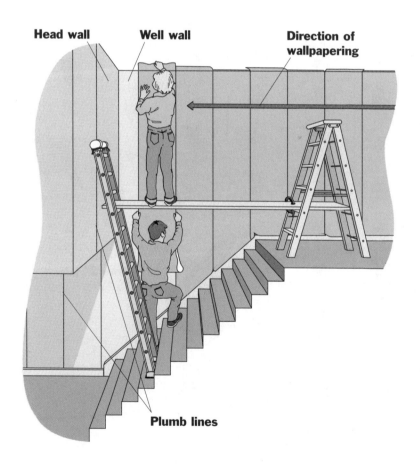

Head wall   Well wall   Direction of wallpapering

Plumb lines

When notching the sheet that overlaps the head wall, allow for a ½-inch tab that extends beyond the corner. Before wallpapering the head wall, lay out the location of each sheet. Avoid any sheet narrower than 6 inches. Complete the inside corner, overlapping the tab with a sheet held back from the corner ¼ inch.

Dormer

Because dormers have so many intersections where mismatches can occur, avoid using large-pattern wallcovering. Begin by hanging the sheets on the wall adjacent to the angled wall, lapping ½ inch at the corner. Draw plumb lines on the angled wall and the knee wall. Cut and hang the sheets for the angled wall first, overlapping the knee wall by ¼ inch.

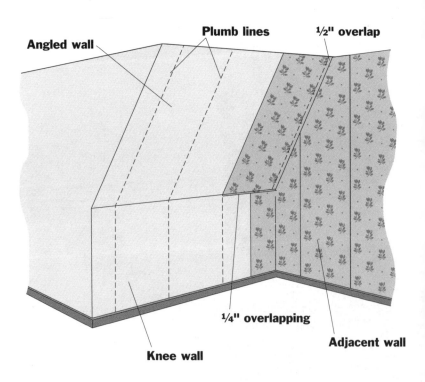

Angled wall

Plumb lines

½" overlap

¼" overlapping

Knee wall

Adjacent wall

Complete the angled wall. With the last sheet, overlap onto the outside wall ½ inch. Cover the knee wall, following the seam lines of the angled wall. Overlap onto the outside wall ½ inch. Next cover the outside wall. Plan the layout of the wall sheet-by-sheet, making sure that no sheet is less than 3 inches wide. Hold back the sheets ¼ inch from the edge to prevent peeling.

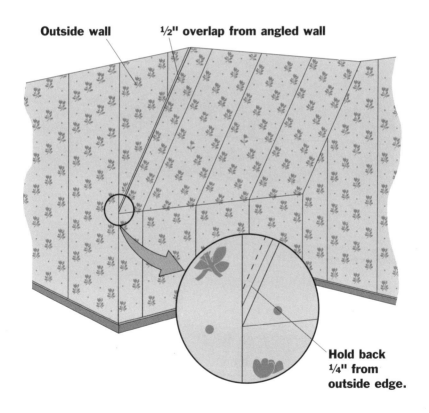

Outside wall

½" overlap from angled wall

Hold back ¼" from outside edge.

5 Ceiling

Although ceilings should be covered before
walls, try to gain some experience wallpapering
walls first. Begin on the ceiling by enlisting
a helper and setting up two stepladders. Decide
which side of the room attracts the most attention and
align the patterns of the ceiling and wall there. Snap chalk
lines for a guide, allowing for a 1-inch overlap onto the
walls. Cut the first sheet 4 inches longer than the length of
the ceiling, then paste and book.

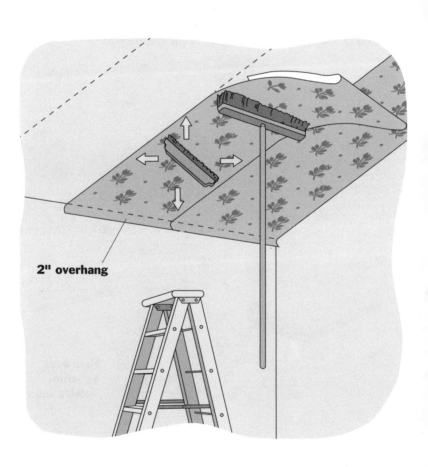

2" overhang

Hang and smooth the material using the same techniques as for walls. Use a soft push broom to hold the material in place as you work. If the walls will be covered, trim the ceiling material so it overhangs the wall ½ inch. If there will be no wallcovering on the walls, push the broad knife into the corner and trim.

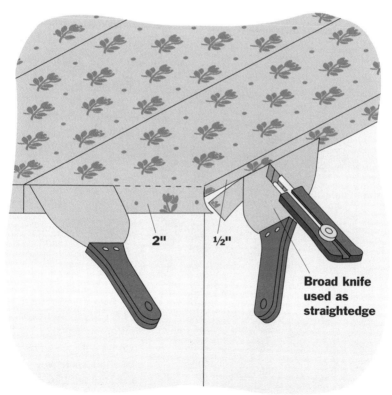

2" **½"**

Broad knife used as straightedge

Trimming technique if wall will not be wallpapered

Trimming technique if wall will be wallpapered

6 Borders

To hang borders, such as a chair-rail border around a room, first snap a level chalk line for reference. Paste and book accordion-style, as with wallcovering sheets. Have a helper unwrap the border (or remove the backing if border is self-adhesive type) as you smooth it in place. If you apply the border above a section of wallcovering, use a lap seam or double-cut seam (see page 37).

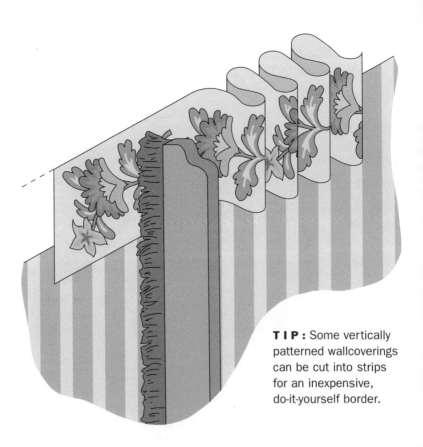

T I P : Some vertically patterned wallcoverings can be cut into strips for an inexpensive, do-it-yourself border.

To make a miter cut at a corner, first apply the sheets, allowing them to run past each other. Position a straight-edge as a guide and make a cut from the inside corner to the outside corner. Cut through both sheets of border in one pass, without scoring the underlying wall. Remove the excess material, smooth the sheets together, and roll the joint with a seam roller.

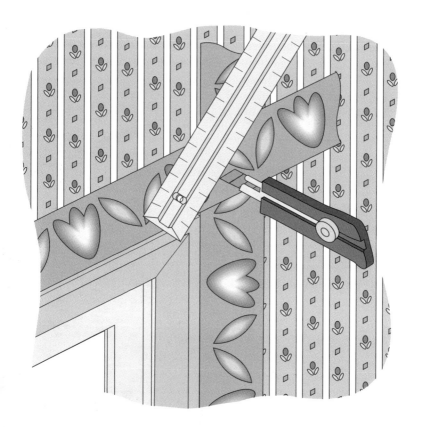

Repairs

1

Fix a seam

Often seams come loose because the paste was not applied evenly all the way to the edge of the material. To repair a loose seam, gently pry open each side of the seam and inject white glue underneath. Push the sheets down and wipe off the excess glue with a damp sponge. Run a seam roller over the spot immediately. Wait a few minutes, wipe, and roll until the seam adheres.

2

Flatten a bubble

To flatten a bubble, make an L-shaped incision. (If possible, cut along a section of the pattern to hide the cut.) Pull back the resulting tab, apply white glue, and smooth down the tab with your hand. Wipe off any excess glue. Check every few minutes until you are sure the spot is secure.

Patch a damaged area

3

For a large damaged area that cannot be reglued, first position a sheet of wallcovering over the spot so it aligns with the pattern. Tape it in place temporarily. Using a straightedge, cut out a rectangle, slicing through both the new and the old wallcovering but not scoring the underlying wall. Lift out the damaged section, clean the wall, and paste the patch in place.

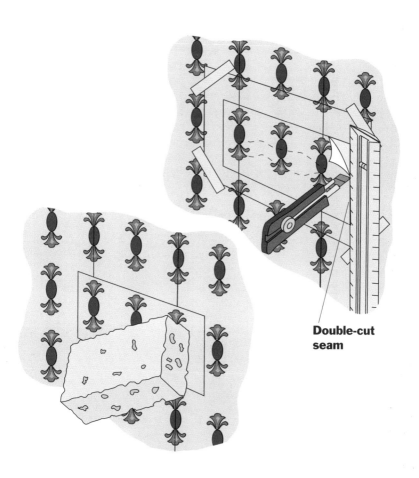

Double-cut seam

U.S./Metric Measure Conversions

	Symbol	**Formulas for Exact Measures**		To find:	**Rounded Measures for Quick Reference**	
		When you know:	Multiply by:			
Mass (Weight)	oz	ounces	28.35	grams	1 oz	= 30 g
	lb	pounds	0.45	kilograms	4 oz	= 115 g
	g	grams	0.035	ounces	8 oz	= 225 g
	kg	kilograms	2.2	pounds	16 oz = 1 lb	= 450 g
					32 oz = 2 lb	= 900 g
					36 oz = $2^1/_4$ lb	= 1000 g (1 kg)
Volume	pt	pints	0.47	liters	1 c	= 250 ml
	qt	quarts	0.95	liters	2 c (1pt)	= 500 ml
	gal	gallons	3.785	liters	4 c (1 qt)	= 1 liter
	ml	milliliters	0.034	fluid ounces	4 qt (1 gal)	= $3^3/_4$ liter
Length	in	inches	2.54	centimeters	$^3/_8$ in	= 1.0 cm
	ft	feet	30.48	centimeters	1 in	= 2.5 cm
	yd	yards	0.9144	meters	2 in	= 5.0 cm
	mi	miles	1.609	kilometers	$2^1/_2$ in	= 6.5 cm
	km	kilometers	0.621	miles	12 in (1 ft)	= 30.0 cm
	m	meters	1.094	yards	1 yd	= 90.0 cm
	cm	centimeters	0.39	inches	100 ft	= 30.0 m
					1 mi	= 1.6 km
Temperature	°F	Fahrenheit	$^5/_9$ (after subtracting 32)	Celsius	32° F	= 0° C
	°C	Celsius	$^9/_5$ (then add 32)	Fahrenheit	212° F	= 100° C
Area	in²	square inches	6.452	square centimeters	1 in²	= 6.5 cm²
	ft²	square feet	929.0	square centimeters	1 ft²	= 930 cm²
	yd²	square yards	8361.0	square centimeters	1 yd²	= 8360 cm²
	a	acres	0.4047	hectares	1 a	= 4050 m²